Contents

My Country

Wednesday, 6 May

Biting
Trawas
East Java
Indonesia 61375

Dear Chris,

Selamat pagi! (You say 'say-LAR-mart PAR-gee'. This means 'hello' in Indonesian.)

My name is Muhammad MasRukhan and I'm 8 years old. I live in the village of Biting, in Indonesia. Biting is on a big island called Java. There are many islands in Indonesia.

Being your penpal is a great idea. I can tell you all about life in Indonesia.

Write back soon!

From

Muhammad

This is me with my mum, dad, and my little sister, Rizki – she's 4 years old.

INDONESIA

David Cumming

Photographs by Julio Etchart

LETTERS FROM AROUND THE WORLD

Titles in this series

A Cherrytree Book

Conceived and produced by

Nutshell
MEDIA
www.nutshellmedialtd.co.uk

First published in paperback in 2009 by
Evans Brothers Ltd
2A Portman Mansions
Chiltern Street
London W1U 6NR

VISIT OUR WEBSITE
Evans
www.evansbooks.co.uk

Editor: Polly Goodman
Design: Mayer Media Ltd
Map artwork: Encompass Graphics Ltd
All other artwork: Mayer Media Ltd

All photographs were taken by Julio Etchart,
except p28: Bernard Napthine/Lonely Planet Images.

Acknowledgements
The photographer would like to thank the MasRukhan
family, the staff and pupils of Seloliman School, East Java,
Indonesia, the staff at PPLH Ecotourism Centre, and Fiona
Smith from VSO, Indonesia, for all their help with this book.

British Library Cataloguing in Publication Data
Cumming, David
    Indonesia. – (Letters from around the world)
    1. Indonesia – Social conditions – Juvenile literature
    2. Indonesia – Social life and customs – Juvenile
       literature
    I. Title
    959.8'038

ISBN 9781842345894

Cover: Muhammad (centre) with his friends (from
   the left) Miftahul, Kholis, Agus and Evi.
Title page: Some of Muhammad's friends enjoying
   a mid-morning rice snack at school.
This page: A view over volcano craters in East Java.
   There are 400 volcanoes in Indonesia.
Contents page: Muhammad's classmate Arti enjoys
   a rice cracker at break time.
Glossary page: Writing sums on the chalkboard.
Further Information page: A farmer ploughs a paddy
   field with the help of two cows.
Index: Villagers from Biting on their way to work.

Indonesia is a long chain of islands between Malaysia and Australia. Some of the islands are too small to live on. Others are among the biggest in the world.

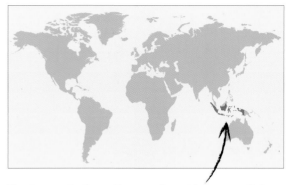

Indonesia's place in the world.

THAILAND

South China Sea

PHILIPPINES

BRUNEI

PACIFIC OCEAN

M A L A Y S I A

SINGAPORE

Equator

Kapuas

Borneo

Sumatra

Sulawesi

Puncak Jaya 5,029m

I N D O N E S I A

Irian Jaya

Java Sea

JAKARTA

Surabaya

Bandung

Java

Biting

Bali

Flores

Malang

EAST TIMOR

Timor

INDIAN OCEAN

N

AUSTRALIA

0   200   400   600   800 kilometres

0   200   400 miles

There are more than 13,600 islands in Indonesia. They stretch from the Indian Ocean to the Pacific Ocean.

Indonesia has few large cities. Most people live in villages like Biting. They grow food crops such as rice, maize or peanuts, or work on plantations growing mahogany trees. Mahogany wood is used to make furniture.

About 300 people live in Biting. The nearest city is Malang, about 150 kilometres away. It takes 90 minutes to get there in a minibus.

Overhead cables bring electricity to houses in Biting.

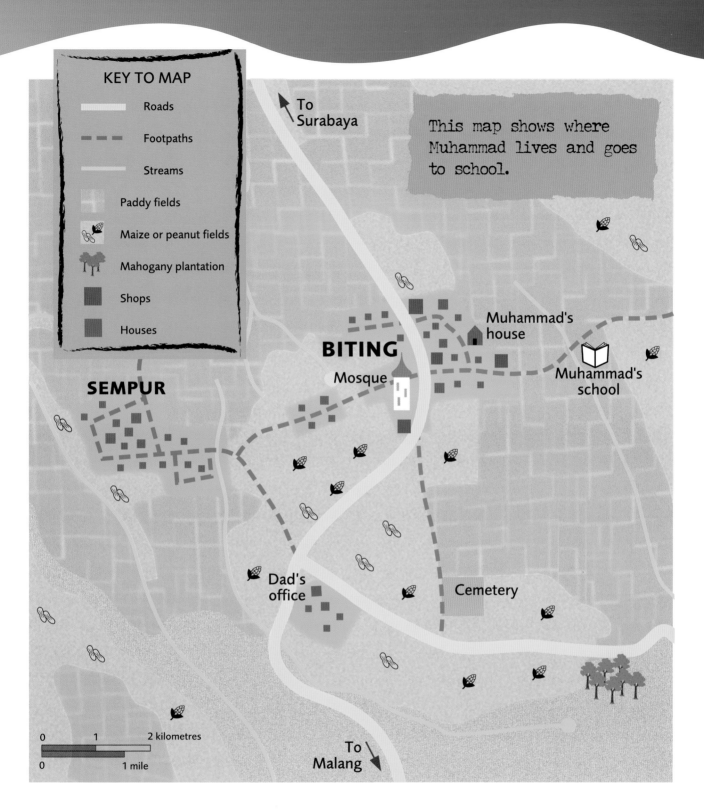

KEY TO MAP

Roads

Footpaths

Streams

Paddy fields

Maize or peanut fields

Mahogany plantation

Shops

Houses

To
Surabaya

This map shows where
Muhammad lives and goes
to school.

BITING

SEMPUR

Mosque

Muhammad's
house

Muhammad's
school

Dad's
office

Cemetery

0   1   2 kilometres

0   1 mile

To
Malang

There is one road that runs through Biting. There
are also many paths. Muhammad walks to school
along a path through the fields. The village has
four small grocery shops and a mosque.

Landscape and Weather

Java is like the rest of Indonesia. It has many forests, hills and mountains, and little low or flat land. Many of the mountains are volcanoes.

Many of Indonesia's farmers dig flat terraces into the hillsides for growing rice.

Indonesia is on the Equator, so it is hot all year round. In East Java, the temperature can reach as high as 36°C. A wind called the monsoon brings a lot of rain between October and April. There is not much rain between May and September.

Mount Bromo is near Biting. It is an active volcano which still erupts.

Biting's Climate

January

Temperature

26°C

300mm Rainfall

July

Temperature

27°C

64mm Rainfall

At Home

Muhammad's home is similar to other houses in Biting. It has brick walls and a wooden roof. The roof sticks out on pillars to keep the house cool. The mosque (see page 27) also has a large roof to stop the inside getting hot.

Muhammad and his family leave their shoes outside the house, which is the custom in Indonesia. It helps to keep the dirt out.

Muhammad's house is on one floor. It has a living room, a kitchen, a bathroom, and a small room for prayers. There are three bedrooms – one for Muhammad, one for his parents and one for Rizki.

Muhammad's family has a TV and video in the living room, but they still spend a lot of time reading.

Washing dries quickly in the hot Indonesian sun.

Muhammad's dad works
hard looking after the
garden and animals.

There is a garden at the back of the house. Muhammad's parents grow fruit and vegetables there. They also grow vegetables in a nearby allotment.

The family owns three ducks and two chickens. Muhammad collects their eggs for his mum to cook.

Muhammad's mum grows
spinach (on the left) and
peanuts (on the right) in
the garden.

Thursday, 12 June

Biting
Trawas
East Java
Indonesia 61375

Dear Chris,

Thanks for your letter. It took over three weeks to get here.
Our village isn't big enough to have a post-van, so Dad had to
pick it up from Malang (150 kilometres away) when he was
last there. All our post is delivered there. How do you get
your letters?

I'm glad you like drawing. It's one of my favourite hobbies,
too. We're learning how to draw maps at school. Today we
drew the area around our houses. Tomorrow we're going to
draw proper maps of Biting. I'm practising at home.

Write again soon!

From

Muhammad

Here I am drawing our
house and the countryside
around it.

Food and Mealtimes

Rice is the most important food in Indonesia. People eat it every day. It is used to make a popular dish called *nasi goreng* (you say 'nar-SEE go-RENG'). The rice is stir-fried in a wok with meat, vegetables and eggs. *Gado-gado* is another favourite. It's a salad covered with peanut sauce.

Every week, a food trader (in red) visits the village on her motorbike to sell vegetables, tofu and fish.

Muhammad's dad collects avocados from trees in his allotment. He uses a net on a pole.

This village woman is peeling the shells from peanuts. The peanuts will be used to make sauces and peanut dishes.

On street stalls you can buy barbecued lamb or chicken on skewers. They are dipped into a spicy shrimp paste, or sauces made from coconut milk, peanuts or soya beans.

For breakfast, Muhammad has rice and fish. Lunch is more rice and fish, along with vegetables and tofu.

In the evening, the family eats stir-fried rice with the leftovers of the day's fish and vegetables.

Friday, 18 July

Biting
Trawas
East Java
Indonesia 61375

Hi Chris,

If you like coconut, why don't you try making some coconut rice?

You will need: 1 cup coconut milk (fresh is best; otherwise tinned),
4 tablespoons grated coconut (fresh if possible; dried if not),
1/2 cup long-grained rice, salt and pepper.

1. Put the rice in a sieve and rinse it well with water.
2. Then put it in a saucepan with the coconut milk.
3. Bring to the boil and simmer for 10 minutes, or until most of the coconut milk has been absorbed. (Mum usually helps me with this.)
4. Mix in the grated coconut and season with a little salt and pepper.

Try it and let me know what you think.

From

Muhammad

Here I am watching Mum stirring the coconut rice.

School Day

Muhammad's school is about 2 kilometres from his home. Most pupils walk there from the villages nearby.

There are 120 pupils in the school, aged between 7 and 11 years old. They all have to wear the school uniform.

It takes Muhammad (left) and his friend Setiawan (centre) about half an hour to get to school. They are joined by other pupils along the way.

This is Muhammad's class in front of the school sign. There are 29 pupils in his class.

Each lesson lasts 40 minutes. The week's timetable is on the wall.

Muhammad only goes to school in the morning. His classes start at 8 a.m. There's a short break at 10.30 a.m. for a snack. School ends at 12.30, when Muhammad goes home for his lunch.

In a maths lesson, children write the sums on the board.

Muhammad's classmate Arti enjoys a rice cracker at break time.

Muhammad studies Indonesian, maths, science, geography and history. Once a week he also learns English.

There are three school terms and one month's holiday during the year.

Tuesday, 19 August

Biting
Trawas
East Java
Indonesia 61375

Dear Chris,

Have I told you about our playground game? Everyone stands in a circle and one person throws a stone in the middle. Each person has to hop to the stone and back in ten hops, then nine hops, then eight, down to one hop. The first person to put their other foot down is out.

What do you play in the playground? Write back and tell me.

From

Muhammad

Here's my class playing a game in the playground.

Off to Work

A farmer ploughs his paddy fields of rice near Biting.

Almost half the people in Indonesia are farmers. They grow rice and other crops. In the cities there are new factories making stereos, computers, clothes and shoes.

Villagers share a ride to work, where they are helping a farmer with his harvest.

Muhammad's dad works for an education centre. He teaches people how to care for the land. He also teaches them to look after the forests. Huge areas of forest are being destroyed every year. Muhammad's dad is trying to stop this.

Here is Muhammad's dad in his office, with the people who work with him.

Free Time

Most people in Indonesia do not have lots of money. Many parents do not have enough money to buy electronic toys for their children. Muhammad is lucky. His parents have a TV and a video. When he's not watching TV, he likes to play football with friends.

Football is Muhammad's favourite sport. He plays with his friends around the village.

These are spectators at the football stadium in Malang. They are watching Arema, Muhammad's favourite team.

Wednesday, 17 September

Biting
Trawas
East Java
Indonesia 61375

Hi Chris,

Your playground game sounds fun.

So, you're a judo whizz-kid! Well, I'm the class arm-wrestling champion. Simply the best! No one comes near beating me. We probably do it a little differently here. Instead of locking hands, we lock wrists and then try to force the other person's hand to the ground. Try it some time. I bet I could beat you!

Bye

Muhammad

My friend Ali is strong, but not as strong as me.

Religion

Like most Indonesians, Muhammad and his family are Muslims. They follow the religion of Islam. After getting up, Muhammad washes and says his prayers. In the evening, too, he washes before praying and going to bed.

A drummer calls villagers to Friday prayers in the mosque.

This is Biting's mosque, the place where Muslims pray.

Friday is Islam's holy day. After school, Muhammad goes to the mosque to pray. Then he goes to the mosque's school. Here he learns Arabic, so that he can read the Qur'an. This is Islam's holy book.

Children read the Qur'an at the *madrasah* (the mosque's school).

Fact File

Capital city: Jakarta is in the west of Java. As well as the capital, Jakarta is Indonesia's biggest city.

Other major cities: Bandung and Surabaya.

Size: 1,919,440km². Indonesia is the fourth-largest country in the world. It has about 13,677 islands. They stretch for 5,100km through 8 million km² of sea, which means that there is more water than land in Indonesia. Only about 1,500 of the islands are inhabited.

Population: About 240 million. There are 362 different peoples in Indonesia.

Flag: The Indonesian flag has a red and a white band. Red stands for courage and white stands for purity.

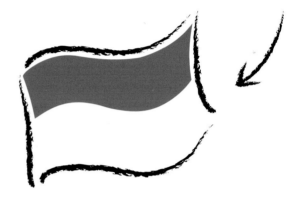

History: The islands of Indonesia were once known as the Spice Islands. European merchants travelled there by ship to buy spices such as cloves and nutmegs.

Languages: Bahasa Indonesia is the official language, which is spoken throughout the country. Other important languages are English and Dutch. There are also 250 local languages, of which Javanese, Sundanese, Malay and Madurese are the most spoken.

Currency: Rupiah (divided into sen). 1 rupiah = 100 sen.

Highest mountain: Puncak Jaya (5,029m), in Irian Jaya.

Rainforest: Indonesia has the world's second-largest area of tropical rainforest. Only Brazil has a bigger area.

Wildlife: The rainforests are home to many different birds, and animals such as orangutans and lizards. The world's largest lizard lives on Komodo island. It can grow up to 3m long and weigh 135kg.

Longest river: The Kapuas (1,142km), in Borneo.

Main religions: Islam is the main religion in Indonesia. About 86 per cent of the people are Muslim. Most other people follow Christianity or Hinduism.

Stamps: Indonesian stamps often show the country's festivals, wildlife and plants.

Glossary

allotment A small area of land used for growing fruit and vegetables.

carp A small freshwater fish that lives in rivers and ponds.

Equator An imaginary line round the middle of the Earth.

erupt To burst open. When a volcano erupts, it throws out lava and gases from inside the earth.

harvest To collect a crop.

Islam A major world faith; the religion of Muslims.

monsoon The name given to a major wind that blows over Indonesia, bringing rain.

maize A cereal crop with large grains that grow in rows on a cob.

mosque The building in which Muslims pray.

paddy field A field where rice is grown.

pillar A tall stone or wooden post that holds something up.

plantation A large area of land where one crop is grown to sell abroad.

Qur'an The holy book of Islam.

rice cracker A big crispy biscuit made from puffed rice fried in oil.

temperature How hot or cold something or someone is.

terrace A flat piece of ground on the side of a hill, like a step.

tofu A food made from soya beans.

volcano A mountain with a hole in the top. It can erupt, throwing out lava and ash through the hole.

wok A deep saucepan with a round bottom. It is used for frying food quickly.

Further Information

Information books:

Exploring Continents: Asia by Anita Ganeri (Heinemann, 2006)

Rainforest Explorer by Greg Pyers (Raintree, 2005)

Step-up Religion: Why is Muhammad Important to Muslims? by Jean Mead (Evans, 2008)

Talking About My Faith: I am Muslim by Cath Senker (Franklin Watts, 2005)

Young Explorer: We're from Indonesia by Vicky Parker (Heinemann, 2006)

World in Focus: Indonesia by Sally Morgan (Wayland, 2007)

A World of Recipes: Indonesia by Julie McCulloch (Heinemann, 2004)

Websites:

CIA World Factbook
www.cia.gov/
Facts and figures about Indonesia and other countries.

Indonesian Home Page
http://indonesia.elga.net.id/
Information about all things Indonesian, including recipes, clothes and traditional games.

Unicef
www.unicef.org/infobycountry/indonesia.html
News, facts and figures about Indonesia.

Index